TEACHER PLANNER

ROCKRIDGE
PRESS

For general information on our other products and services or to obtain technical support, please contact our Customer Care Department within the United States at (866) 744-2665, or outside the United States at (510) 253-0500.

Rockridge Press publishes its books in a variety of electronic and print formats. Some content that appears in print may not be available in electronic books, and vice versa.

Interior and Cover Designer: Richard Tapp
Art Producer: Sue Smith
Editor: Erum Khan
Production Editor: Mia Moran

Cover Illustration ©Clarice Gifford, 2019

ISBN: Print 978-1-64611-329-3

RO

Name

School

Subjects / Grades

Room

The ______ to ______ School Year at a Glance

Student Information

NAME	BIRTHDAY	PARENT/GUARDIAN

PHONE	EMAIL	NOTES

STUDENT INFO

Important Dates

JULY

4th Independence Day

☆
☆
☆
☆
☆
☆
☆
☆

AUGUST

9th Book Lovers Day

☆
☆
☆
☆
☆
☆
☆
☆

SEPTEMBER

Labor Day *(first Monday)*

24th National Punctuation Day

☆
☆
☆
☆
☆
☆
☆
☆

OCTOBER

World Smile Day *(first Friday)*

Columbus Day / Indigenous Peoples' Day *(second Monday)*

31st Halloween

☆
☆
☆
☆
☆
☆
☆
☆

NOVEMBER

11th Veterans Day

23rd Fibonacci Day

Thanksgiving *(fourth Thursday)*

☆
☆
☆
☆
☆
☆
☆
☆

DECEMBER

Hanukkah *(Hebrew calendar)*

26th to January 1st Kwanzaa

24th Christmas Eve

25th Christmas Day

31st New Year's Eve

☆
☆
☆
☆
☆
☆
☆
☆

IMPORTANT DATES

JANUARY

1st New Year's Day

4th National Trivia Day

Martin Luther King Jr. Day *(third Monday)*

☆
☆
☆
☆
☆
☆
☆
☆

FEBRUARY

Black History Month

14th Valentine's Day

Presidents Day *(third Monday)*

☆
☆
☆
☆
☆
☆
☆
☆

MARCH

Women's History Month

17th Saint Patrick's Day

Holi *(lunar calendar)*

☆
☆
☆
☆
☆
☆
☆
☆

APRIL

1st April Fools' Day

22nd Earth Day

☆
☆
☆
☆
☆
☆
☆
☆

MAY

Teacher Appreciation Week *(first week)*

5th Cinco de Mayo

Mother's Day *(second Sunday)*

Memorial Day *(last Monday)*

☆
☆
☆
☆
☆
☆
☆
☆

JUNE

Father's Day *(third Sunday)*

☆
☆
☆
☆
☆
☆
☆
☆

July

Year ______

SUNDAY	MONDAY	TUESDAY	WEDNESDAY

"Positive anything is better than negative nothing."
• Elbert Hubbard

THURSDAY	FRIDAY	SATURDAY

NOTES

JULY

Week of ___/___/___ to ___/___/___

	MONDAY	TUESDAY	WEDNESDAY
1	☐ ☐ ☐ ☐ ☐ ☐	☐ ☐ ☐ ☐ ☐ ☐	☐ ☐ ☐ ☐ ☐ ☐
2	☐ ☐ ☐ ☐ ☐ ☐	☐ ☐ ☐ ☐ ☐ ☐	☐ ☐ ☐ ☐ ☐ ☐
3	☐ ☐ ☐ ☐ ☐ ☐	☐ ☐ ☐ ☐ ☐ ☐	☐ ☐ ☐ ☐ ☐ ☐
4	☐ ☐ ☐ ☐ ☐ ☐	☐ ☐ ☐ ☐ ☐ ☐	☐ ☐ ☐ ☐ ☐ ☐
5	☐ ☐ ☐ ☐ ☐ ☐	☐ ☐ ☐ ☐ ☐ ☐	☐ ☐ ☐ ☐ ☐ ☐
6	☐ ☐ ☐ ☐ ☐ ☐	☐ ☐ ☐ ☐ ☐ ☐	☐ ☐ ☐ ☐ ☐ ☐

THURSDAY	FRIDAY
☐	☐
☐	☐
☐	☐
☐	☐
☐	☐
☐	☐
☐	☐
☐	☐
☐	☐
☐	☐
☐	☐
☐	☐
☐	☐
☐	☐
☐	☐
☐	☐
☐	☐
☐	☐
☐	☐
☐	☐
☐	☐
☐	☐
☐	☐
☐	☐
☐	☐
☐	☐
☐	☐
☐	☐
☐	☐
☐	☐
☐	☐
☐	☐
☐	☐
☐	☐
☐	☐
☐	☐

NOTES

Week of ___/___/___ to ___/___/___

MONDAY	TUESDAY	WEDNESDAY

JULY

SUBJECTS

"The giving of love is an education in itself."
• Eleanor Roosevelt

THURSDAY	FRIDAY

NOTES

JULY

Week of __/__/__ to __/__/__

MONDAY	TUESDAY	WEDNESDAY

JULY

SUBJECTS

THURSDAY	FRIDAY
☐	☐
☐	☐
☐	☐
☐	☐
☐	☐
☐	☐
☐	☐
☐	☐
☐	☐
☐	☐
☐	☐
☐	☐
☐	☐
☐	☐
☐	☐
☐	☐
☐	☐
☐	☐
☐	☐
☐	☐
☐	☐
☐	☐
☐	☐
☐	☐
☐	☐
☐	☐
☐	☐
☐	☐
☐	☐
☐	☐
☐	☐
☐	☐
☐	☐
☐	☐
☐	☐
☐	☐

NOTES

Week of ___/___/___ to ___/___/___

MONDAY	TUESDAY	WEDNESDAY

JULY

SUBJECTS

THURSDAY	FRIDAY

NOTES

JULY

August

Year

SUNDAY	MONDAY	TUESDAY	WEDNESDAY

AUGUST

"Our lives are defined by opportunities, even the ones we miss."

• Eric Roth

THURSDAY	FRIDAY	SATURDAY

NOTES

AUGUST

Week of ___ /___ /___ to ___ /___ /___

MONDAY	TUESDAY	WEDNESDAY
☐ ☐ ☐ ☐ ☐ ☐	☐ ☐ ☐ ☐ ☐ ☐	☐ ☐ ☐ ☐ ☐ ☐
☐ ☐ ☐ ☐ ☐ ☐	☐ ☐ ☐ ☐ ☐ ☐	☐ ☐ ☐ ☐ ☐ ☐
☐ ☐ ☐ ☐ ☐ ☐	☐ ☐ ☐ ☐ ☐ ☐	☐ ☐ ☐ ☐ ☐ ☐
☐ ☐ ☐ ☐ ☐ ☐	☐ ☐ ☐ ☐ ☐ ☐	☐ ☐ ☐ ☐ ☐ ☐
☐ ☐ ☐ ☐ ☐ ☐	☐ ☐ ☐ ☐ ☐ ☐	☐ ☐ ☐ ☐ ☐ ☐
☐ ☐ ☐ ☐ ☐ ☐	☐ ☐ ☐ ☐ ☐ ☐	☐ ☐ ☐ ☐ ☐ ☐

THURSDAY	FRIDAY

NOTES

AUGUST

Week of ___/___/___ to ___/___/___

MONDAY	TUESDAY	WEDNESDAY
☐	☐	☐

AUGUST

SUBJECTS

"A leader takes people where they want to go. A great leader takes people where they don't necessarily want to go, but ought to be."

• Rosalynn Carter

THURSDAY	FRIDAY
☐	☐
☐	☐
☐	☐
☐	☐
☐	☐
☐	☐
☐	☐
☐	☐
☐	☐
☐	☐
☐	☐
☐	☐
☐	☐
☐	☐
☐	☐
☐	☐
☐	☐
☐	☐
☐	☐
☐	☐
☐	☐
☐	☐
☐	☐
☐	☐
☐	☐
☐	☐
☐	☐
☐	☐
☐	☐
☐	☐
☐	☐
☐	☐
☐	☐
☐	☐
☐	☐
☐	☐

NOTES

Week of ___/___/___ to ___/___/___

MONDAY	TUESDAY	WEDNESDAY

AUGUST

SUBJECTS

THURSDAY	FRIDAY
☐	☐
☐	☐
☐	☐
☐	☐
☐	☐
☐	☐
☐	☐
☐	☐
☐	☐
☐	☐
☐	☐
☐	☐
☐	☐
☐	☐
☐	☐
☐	☐
☐	☐
☐	☐
☐	☐
☐	☐
☐	☐
☐	☐
☐	☐
☐	☐
☐	☐
☐	☐
☐	☐
☐	☐
☐	☐
☐	☐
☐	☐
☐	☐
☐	☐
☐	☐
☐	☐
☐	☐

NOTES

Week of __/__/__ to __/__/__

MONDAY	TUESDAY	WEDNESDAY
1		
2		
3		
4		
5		
6		

AUGUST

SUBJECTS

THURSDAY	FRIDAY

NOTES

September

Year

SUNDAY	MONDAY	TUESDAY	WEDNESDAY

"Feet, what do I need you for when I have wings to fly?"
• Frida Kahlo

THURSDAY	FRIDAY	SATURDAY

NOTES

SEPTEMBER

Week of ___/___/___ to ___/___/___

SEPTEMBER

	MONDAY	TUESDAY	WEDNESDAY
1	☐ ☐ ☐ ☐ ☐ ☐	☐ ☐ ☐ ☐ ☐ ☐	☐ ☐ ☐ ☐ ☐ ☐
2	☐ ☐ ☐ ☐ ☐ ☐	☐ ☐ ☐ ☐ ☐ ☐	☐ ☐ ☐ ☐ ☐ ☐
3	☐ ☐ ☐ ☐ ☐ ☐	☐ ☐ ☐ ☐ ☐ ☐	☐ ☐ ☐ ☐ ☐ ☐
4	☐ ☐ ☐ ☐ ☐ ☐	☐ ☐ ☐ ☐ ☐ ☐	☐ ☐ ☐ ☐ ☐ ☐
5	☐ ☐ ☐ ☐ ☐ ☐	☐ ☐ ☐ ☐ ☐ ☐	☐ ☐ ☐ ☐ ☐ ☐
6	☐ ☐ ☐ ☐ ☐ ☐	☐ ☐ ☐ ☐ ☐ ☐	☐ ☐ ☐ ☐ ☐ ☐

THURSDAY	FRIDAY

NOTES

Week of ___/___/___ to ___/___/___

MONDAY	TUESDAY	WEDNESDAY

SEPTEMBER

"Do not wait for leaders; do it alone, person to person. Be faithful in small things because it is in them that your strength lies."

• Mother Teresa

THURSDAY	FRIDAY
☐	☐
☐	☐
☐	☐
☐	☐
☐	☐
☐	☐
☐	☐
☐	☐
☐	☐
☐	☐
☐	☐
☐	☐
☐	☐
☐	☐
☐	☐
☐	☐
☐	☐
☐	☐
☐	☐
☐	☐
☐	☐
☐	☐
☐	☐
☐	☐
☐	☐
☐	☐
☐	☐
☐	☐
☐	☐
☐	☐
☐	☐
☐	☐
☐	☐
☐	☐
☐	☐
☐	☐

NOTES

Week of __/__/__ to __/__/__

	MONDAY	TUESDAY	WEDNESDAY
1			
2			
3			
4			
5			
6			

THURSDAY	FRIDAY

NOTES

SEPTEMBER

Week of ___/___/___ to ___/___/___

MONDAY	TUESDAY	WEDNESDAY
☐	☐	☐

SEPTEMBER

THURSDAY	FRIDAY
☐	☐
☐	☐
☐	☐
☐	☐
☐	☐
☐	☐
☐	☐
☐	☐
☐	☐
☐	☐
☐	☐
☐	☐
☐	☐
☐	☐
☐	☐
☐	☐
☐	☐
☐	☐
☐	☐
☐	☐
☐	☐
☐	☐
☐	☐
☐	☐
☐	☐
☐	☐
☐	☐
☐	☐
☐	☐
☐	☐
☐	☐
☐	☐
☐	☐
☐	☐
☐	☐
☐	☐

NOTES

Week of ___/___/___ to ___/___/___

	MONDAY	TUESDAY	WEDNESDAY
1	☐ ☐ ☐ ☐ ☐ ☐	☐ ☐ ☐ ☐ ☐ ☐	☐ ☐ ☐ ☐ ☐ ☐
2	☐ ☐ ☐ ☐ ☐ ☐	☐ ☐ ☐ ☐ ☐ ☐	☐ ☐ ☐ ☐ ☐ ☐
3	☐ ☐ ☐ ☐ ☐ ☐	☐ ☐ ☐ ☐ ☐ ☐	☐ ☐ ☐ ☐ ☐ ☐
4	☐ ☐ ☐ ☐ ☐ ☐	☐ ☐ ☐ ☐ ☐ ☐	☐ ☐ ☐ ☐ ☐ ☐
5	☐ ☐ ☐ ☐ ☐ ☐	☐ ☐ ☐ ☐ ☐ ☐	☐ ☐ ☐ ☐ ☐ ☐
6	☐ ☐ ☐ ☐ ☐ ☐	☐ ☐ ☐ ☐ ☐ ☐	☐ ☐ ☐ ☐ ☐ ☐

THURSDAY	FRIDAY
☐	☐
☐	☐
☐	☐
☐	☐
☐	☐
☐	☐
☐	☐
☐	☐
☐	☐
☐	☐
☐	☐
☐	☐
☐	☐
☐	☐
☐	☐
☐	☐
☐	☐
☐	☐
☐	☐
☐	☐
☐	☐
☐	☐
☐	☐
☐	☐
☐	☐
☐	☐
☐	☐
☐	☐
☐	☐
☐	☐
☐	☐
☐	☐
☐	☐
☐	☐
☐	☐
☐	☐

NOTES

SEPTEMBER

October

Year

SUNDAY	MONDAY	TUESDAY	WEDNESDAY

OCTOBER

"To live is so startling it leaves little time for anything else."
• Emily Dickinson

THURSDAY	FRIDAY	SATURDAY

NOTES

Week of ___/___/___ to ___/___/___

	MONDAY	TUESDAY	WEDNESDAY
1			
2			
3			
4			
5			
6			

OCTOBER

SUBJECTS

THURSDAY	FRIDAY

NOTES

Week of ___/___/___ to ___/___/___

	MONDAY	TUESDAY	WEDNESDAY
1	☐ ☐ ☐ ☐ ☐ ☐	☐ ☐ ☐ ☐ ☐ ☐	☐ ☐ ☐ ☐ ☐ ☐
2	☐ ☐ ☐ ☐ ☐ ☐	☐ ☐ ☐ ☐ ☐ ☐	☐ ☐ ☐ ☐ ☐ ☐
3	☐ ☐ ☐ ☐ ☐ ☐	☐ ☐ ☐ ☐ ☐ ☐	☐ ☐ ☐ ☐ ☐ ☐
4	☐ ☐ ☐ ☐ ☐ ☐	☐ ☐ ☐ ☐ ☐ ☐	☐ ☐ ☐ ☐ ☐ ☐
5	☐ ☐ ☐ ☐ ☐ ☐	☐ ☐ ☐ ☐ ☐ ☐	☐ ☐ ☐ ☐ ☐ ☐
6	☐ ☐ ☐ ☐ ☐ ☐	☐ ☐ ☐ ☐ ☐ ☐	☐ ☐ ☐ ☐ ☐ ☐

"If your actions inspire others to dream more, learn more, do more, and become more, you are a leader."

• John Quincy Adams

THURSDAY	FRIDAY
☐	☐
☐	☐
☐	☐
☐	☐
☐	☐
☐	☐
☐	☐
☐	☐
☐	☐
☐	☐
☐	☐
☐	☐
☐	☐
☐	☐
☐	☐
☐	☐
☐	☐
☐	☐
☐	☐
☐	☐
☐	☐
☐	☐
☐	☐
☐	☐
☐	☐
☐	☐
☐	☐
☐	☐
☐	☐
☐	☐
☐	☐
☐	☐
☐	☐
☐	☐
☐	☐
☐	☐

NOTES

OCTOBER

Week of ___/___/___ to ___/___/___

	MONDAY	TUESDAY	WEDNESDAY
1	☐ ☐ ☐ ☐ ☐ ☐	☐ ☐ ☐ ☐ ☐ ☐	☐ ☐ ☐ ☐ ☐ ☐
2	☐ ☐ ☐ ☐ ☐ ☐	☐ ☐ ☐ ☐ ☐ ☐	☐ ☐ ☐ ☐ ☐ ☐
3	☐ ☐ ☐ ☐ ☐ ☐	☐ ☐ ☐ ☐ ☐ ☐	☐ ☐ ☐ ☐ ☐ ☐
4	☐ ☐ ☐ ☐ ☐ ☐	☐ ☐ ☐ ☐ ☐ ☐	☐ ☐ ☐ ☐ ☐ ☐
5	☐ ☐ ☐ ☐ ☐ ☐	☐ ☐ ☐ ☐ ☐ ☐	☐ ☐ ☐ ☐ ☐ ☐
6	☐ ☐ ☐ ☐ ☐ ☐	☐ ☐ ☐ ☐ ☐ ☐	☐ ☐ ☐ ☐ ☐ ☐

THURSDAY	FRIDAY
☐	☐
☐	☐
☐	☐
☐	☐
☐	☐
☐	☐
☐	☐
☐	☐
☐	☐
☐	☐
☐	☐
☐	☐
☐	☐
☐	☐
☐	☐
☐	☐
☐	☐
☐	☐
☐	☐
☐	☐
☐	☐
☐	☐
☐	☐
☐	☐
☐	☐
☐	☐
☐	☐
☐	☐
☐	☐
☐	☐
☐	☐
☐	☐
☐	☐
☐	☐
☐	☐
☐	☐

NOTES

OCTOBER

Week of ___ /___ /___ to ___ /___ /___

	MONDAY	TUESDAY	WEDNESDAY
1			
2			
3			
4			
5			
6			

OCTOBER

SUBJECTS

THURSDAY	FRIDAY

NOTES

OCTOBER

November

Year ____________

SUNDAY	MONDAY	TUESDAY	WEDNESDAY

"If one is lucky, a solitary fantasy can totally transform one million realities."

• Maya Angelou

THURSDAY	FRIDAY	SATURDAY

NOTES

NOVEMBER

Week of ___/___/___ to ___/___/___

	MONDAY	TUESDAY	WEDNESDAY
1	☐ ☐ ☐ ☐ ☐ ☐	☐ ☐ ☐ ☐ ☐ ☐	☐ ☐ ☐ ☐ ☐ ☐
2	☐ ☐ ☐ ☐ ☐ ☐	☐ ☐ ☐ ☐ ☐ ☐	☐ ☐ ☐ ☐ ☐ ☐
3	☐ ☐ ☐ ☐ ☐ ☐	☐ ☐ ☐ ☐ ☐ ☐	☐ ☐ ☐ ☐ ☐ ☐
4	☐ ☐ ☐ ☐ ☐ ☐	☐ ☐ ☐ ☐ ☐ ☐	☐ ☐ ☐ ☐ ☐ ☐
5	☐ ☐ ☐ ☐ ☐ ☐	☐ ☐ ☐ ☐ ☐ ☐	☐ ☐ ☐ ☐ ☐ ☐
6	☐ ☐ ☐ ☐ ☐ ☐	☐ ☐ ☐ ☐ ☐ ☐	☐ ☐ ☐ ☐ ☐ ☐

THURSDAY	FRIDAY
☐	☐
☐	☐
☐	☐
☐	☐
☐	☐
☐	☐
☐	☐
☐	☐
☐	☐
☐	☐
☐	☐
☐	☐
☐	☐
☐	☐
☐	☐
☐	☐
☐	☐
☐	☐
☐	☐
☐	☐
☐	☐
☐	☐
☐	☐
☐	☐
☐	☐
☐	☐
☐	☐
☐	☐
☐	☐
☐	☐
☐	☐
☐	☐
☐	☐
☐	☐
☐	☐
☐	☐

NOTES

Week of ___/___/___ to ___/___/___

	MONDAY	TUESDAY	WEDNESDAY
1			
2			
3			
4			
5			
6			

NOVEMBER

"Knowing is not enough; we must apply. Willing is not enough; we must do."

• Johann Wolfgang von Goethe

THURSDAY	FRIDAY
☐	☐
☐	☐
☐	☐
☐	☐
☐	☐
☐	☐
☐	☐
☐	☐
☐	☐
☐	☐
☐	☐
☐	☐
☐	☐
☐	☐
☐	☐
☐	☐
☐	☐
☐	☐
☐	☐
☐	☐
☐	☐
☐	☐
☐	☐
☐	☐
☐	☐
☐	☐
☐	☐
☐	☐
☐	☐
☐	☐
☐	☐
☐	☐
☐	☐
☐	☐
☐	☐
☐	☐

NOTES

Week of ___/___/___ to ___/___/___

	MONDAY	TUESDAY	WEDNESDAY
1	☐ ☐ ☐ ☐ ☐ ☐	☐ ☐ ☐ ☐ ☐ ☐	☐ ☐ ☐ ☐ ☐ ☐
2	☐ ☐ ☐ ☐ ☐ ☐	☐ ☐ ☐ ☐ ☐ ☐	☐ ☐ ☐ ☐ ☐ ☐
3	☐ ☐ ☐ ☐ ☐ ☐	☐ ☐ ☐ ☐ ☐ ☐	☐ ☐ ☐ ☐ ☐ ☐
4	☐ ☐ ☐ ☐ ☐ ☐	☐ ☐ ☐ ☐ ☐ ☐	☐ ☐ ☐ ☐ ☐ ☐
5	☐ ☐ ☐ ☐ ☐ ☐	☐ ☐ ☐ ☐ ☐ ☐	☐ ☐ ☐ ☐ ☐ ☐
6	☐ ☐ ☐ ☐ ☐ ☐	☐ ☐ ☐ ☐ ☐ ☐	☐ ☐ ☐ ☐ ☐ ☐

THURSDAY	FRIDAY
☐	☐
☐	☐
☐	☐
☐	☐
☐	☐
☐	☐
☐	☐
☐	☐
☐	☐
☐	☐
☐	☐
☐	☐
☐	☐
☐	☐
☐	☐
☐	☐
☐	☐
☐	☐
☐	☐
☐	☐
☐	☐
☐	☐
☐	☐
☐	☐
☐	☐
☐	☐
☐	☐
☐	☐
☐	☐
☐	☐
☐	☐
☐	☐
☐	☐
☐	☐
☐	☐
☐	☐

NOTES

Week of ___/___/___ to ___/___/___

	MONDAY	TUESDAY	WEDNESDAY
1			
2			
3			
4			
5			
6			

THURSDAY	FRIDAY
☐	☐
☐	☐
☐	☐
☐	☐
☐	☐
☐	☐
☐	☐
☐	☐
☐	☐
☐	☐
☐	☐
☐	☐
☐	☐
☐	☐
☐	☐
☐	☐
☐	☐
☐	☐
☐	☐
☐	☐
☐	☐
☐	☐
☐	☐
☐	☐
☐	☐
☐	☐
☐	☐
☐	☐
☐	☐
☐	☐
☐	☐
☐	☐
☐	☐
☐	☐
☐	☐
☐	☐

NOTES

December

Year

SUNDAY	MONDAY	TUESDAY	WEDNESDAY

DECEMBER

"Never doubt that a small group of thoughtful, committed citizens can change the world; indeed, it is the only thing that ever has."

•Margaret Mead

THURSDAY	FRIDAY	SATURDAY

NOTES

DECEMBER

Week of ___/___/___ to ___/___/___

	MONDAY	TUESDAY	WEDNESDAY
1			
2			
3			
4			
5			
6			

DECEMBER

SUBJECTS

THURSDAY	FRIDAY

NOTES

DECEMBER

Week of ___/___/___ to ___/___/___

	MONDAY	TUESDAY	WEDNESDAY
1	☐ ☐ ☐ ☐ ☐ ☐	☐ ☐ ☐ ☐ ☐ ☐	☐ ☐ ☐ ☐ ☐ ☐
2	☐ ☐ ☐ ☐ ☐ ☐	☐ ☐ ☐ ☐ ☐ ☐	☐ ☐ ☐ ☐ ☐ ☐
3	☐ ☐ ☐ ☐ ☐ ☐	☐ ☐ ☐ ☐ ☐ ☐	☐ ☐ ☐ ☐ ☐ ☐
4	☐ ☐ ☐ ☐ ☐ ☐	☐ ☐ ☐ ☐ ☐ ☐	☐ ☐ ☐ ☐ ☐ ☐
5	☐ ☐ ☐ ☐ ☐ ☐	☐ ☐ ☐ ☐ ☐ ☐	☐ ☐ ☐ ☐ ☐ ☐
6	☐ ☐ ☐ ☐ ☐ ☐	☐ ☐ ☐ ☐ ☐ ☐	☐ ☐ ☐ ☐ ☐ ☐

"Beware of missing chances; otherwise it may be altogether too late some day."

• Franz Liszt

THURSDAY	FRIDAY
☐	☐
☐	☐
☐	☐
☐	☐
☐	☐
☐	☐
☐	☐
☐	☐
☐	☐
☐	☐
☐	☐
☐	☐
☐	☐
☐	☐
☐	☐
☐	☐
☐	☐
☐	☐
☐	☐
☐	☐
☐	☐
☐	☐
☐	☐
☐	☐
☐	☐
☐	☐
☐	☐
☐	☐
☐	☐
☐	☐
☐	☐
☐	☐
☐	☐
☐	☐
☐	☐
☐	☐

NOTES

DECEMBER

Week of ___/___/___ to ___/___/___

	MONDAY	TUESDAY	WEDNESDAY
1			
2			
3			
4			
5			
6			

THURSDAY	FRIDAY

NOTES

DECEMBER

Week of ___/___/___ to ___/___/___

	MONDAY	TUESDAY	WEDNESDAY
1	☐ ☐ ☐ ☐ ☐ ☐	☐ ☐ ☐ ☐ ☐ ☐	☐ ☐ ☐ ☐ ☐ ☐
2	☐ ☐ ☐ ☐ ☐ ☐	☐ ☐ ☐ ☐ ☐ ☐	☐ ☐ ☐ ☐ ☐ ☐
3	☐ ☐ ☐ ☐ ☐ ☐	☐ ☐ ☐ ☐ ☐ ☐	☐ ☐ ☐ ☐ ☐ ☐
4	☐ ☐ ☐ ☐ ☐ ☐	☐ ☐ ☐ ☐ ☐ ☐	☐ ☐ ☐ ☐ ☐ ☐
5	☐ ☐ ☐ ☐ ☐ ☐	☐ ☐ ☐ ☐ ☐ ☐	☐ ☐ ☐ ☐ ☐ ☐
6	☐ ☐ ☐ ☐ ☐ ☐	☐ ☐ ☐ ☐ ☐ ☐	☐ ☐ ☐ ☐ ☐ ☐

THURSDAY	FRIDAY
☐	☐
☐	☐
☐	☐
☐	☐
☐	☐
☐	☐
☐	☐
☐	☐
☐	☐
☐	☐
☐	☐
☐	☐
☐	☐
☐	☐
☐	☐
☐	☐
☐	☐
☐	☐
☐	☐
☐	☐
☐	☐
☐	☐
☐	☐
☐	☐
☐	☐
☐	☐
☐	☐
☐	☐
☐	☐
☐	☐
☐	☐
☐	☐
☐	☐
☐	☐
☐	☐
☐	☐

NOTES

January

Year ____________________

SUNDAY	MONDAY	TUESDAY	WEDNESDAY

JANUARY

"Never do things others can do and will do, if there are things others cannot do or will not do."

• Amelia Earhart

THURSDAY	FRIDAY	SATURDAY

NOTES

JANUARY

Week of ___/___/___ to ___/___/___

MONDAY	TUESDAY	WEDNESDAY
☐	☐	☐

THURSDAY	FRIDAY
☐	☐
☐	☐
☐	☐
☐	☐
☐	☐
☐	☐
☐	☐
☐	☐
☐	☐
☐	☐
☐	☐
☐	☐
☐	☐
☐	☐
☐	☐
☐	☐
☐	☐
☐	☐
☐	☐
☐	☐
☐	☐
☐	☐
☐	☐
☐	☐
☐	☐
☐	☐
☐	☐
☐	☐
☐	☐
☐	☐
☐	☐
☐	☐
☐	☐
☐	☐
☐	☐
☐	☐

NOTES

Week of ___/___/___ to ___/___/___

MONDAY	TUESDAY	WEDNESDAY
☐	☐	☐
☐	☐	☐
☐	☐	☐
☐	☐	☐
☐	☐	☐
☐	☐	☐

JANUARY

"You manage things; you lead people."
• Grace Murray Hopper

THURSDAY

☐
☐
☐
☐
☐
☐

☐
☐
☐
☐
☐
☐

☐
☐
☐
☐
☐
☐

☐
☐
☐
☐
☐
☐

☐
☐
☐
☐
☐
☐

☐
☐
☐
☐
☐
☐

FRIDAY

☐
☐
☐
☐
☐
☐

☐
☐
☐
☐
☐
☐

☐
☐
☐
☐
☐
☐

☐
☐
☐
☐
☐
☐

☐
☐
☐
☐
☐
☐

☐
☐
☐
☐
☐
☐

NOTES

Week of ___/___/___ to ___/___/___

MONDAY	TUESDAY	WEDNESDAY

JANUARY

SUBJECTS

THURSDAY

FRIDAY

NOTES

Week of ___/___/___ to ___/___/___

MONDAY	TUESDAY	WEDNESDAY
☐	☐	☐
☐	☐	☐
☐	☐	☐
☐	☐	☐
☐	☐	☐
☐	☐	☐

THURSDAY

FRIDAY

NOTES

JANUARY

February

Year ______

SUNDAY	MONDAY	TUESDAY	WEDNESDAY

FEBRUARY

"When one door of happiness closes, another opens; but often we look so long at the closed door that we do not see the one which has been opened for us."

• Helen Keller

THURSDAY	FRIDAY	SATURDAY

NOTES

Week of ___/___/___ to ___/___/___

MONDAY	TUESDAY	WEDNESDAY
☐	☐	☐
☐	☐	☐
☐	☐	☐
☐	☐	☐
☐	☐	☐
☐	☐	☐

FEBRUARY

SUBJECTS

THURSDAY

FRIDAY

NOTES

FEBRUARY

Week of ___/___/___ to ___/___/___

MONDAY	TUESDAY	WEDNESDAY

"The mind is not a vessel to be filled but a fire to be kindled."
• Plutarch

THURSDAY	FRIDAY
☐	☐
☐	☐
☐	☐
☐	☐
☐	☐
☐	☐
☐	☐
☐	☐
☐	☐
☐	☐
☐	☐
☐	☐
☐	☐
☐	☐
☐	☐
☐	☐
☐	☐
☐	☐
☐	☐
☐	☐
☐	☐
☐	☐
☐	☐
☐	☐
☐	☐
☐	☐
☐	☐
☐	☐
☐	☐
☐	☐
☐	☐
☐	☐
☐	☐
☐	☐
☐	☐
☐	☐

NOTES

Week of ___/___/___ to ___/___/___

MONDAY	TUESDAY	WEDNESDAY
☐	☐	☐
☐	☐	☐
☐	☐	☐
☐	☐	☐
☐	☐	☐
☐	☐	☐
☐	☐	☐
☐	☐	☐
☐	☐	☐
☐	☐	☐
☐	☐	☐
☐	☐	☐
☐	☐	☐
☐	☐	☐
☐	☐	☐
☐	☐	☐
☐	☐	☐
☐	☐	☐
☐	☐	☐
☐	☐	☐
☐	☐	☐
☐	☐	☐
☐	☐	☐
☐	☐	☐
☐	☐	☐
☐	☐	☐
☐	☐	☐
☐	☐	☐
☐	☐	☐
☐	☐	☐
☐	☐	☐
☐	☐	☐
☐	☐	☐
☐	☐	☐
☐	☐	☐
☐	☐	☐

THURSDAY

FRIDAY

NOTES

Week of ___/___/___ to ___/___/___

MONDAY	TUESDAY	WEDNESDAY
☐	☐	☐
☐	☐	☐
☐	☐	☐
☐	☐	☐
☐	☐	☐
☐	☐	☐
☐	☐	☐
☐	☐	☐
☐	☐	☐
☐	☐	☐
☐	☐	☐
☐	☐	☐
☐	☐	☐
☐	☐	☐
☐	☐	☐
☐	☐	☐
☐	☐	☐
☐	☐	☐
☐	☐	☐
☐	☐	☐
☐	☐	☐
☐	☐	☐
☐	☐	☐
☐	☐	☐
☐	☐	☐
☐	☐	☐
☐	☐	☐
☐	☐	☐
☐	☐	☐
☐	☐	☐
☐	☐	☐
☐	☐	☐
☐	☐	☐
☐	☐	☐
☐	☐	☐
☐	☐	☐

THURSDAY	FRIDAY
☐	☐
☐	☐
☐	☐
☐	☐
☐	☐
☐	☐
☐	☐
☐	☐
☐	☐
☐	☐
☐	☐
☐	☐
☐	☐
☐	☐
☐	☐
☐	☐
☐	☐
☐	☐
☐	☐
☐	☐
☐	☐
☐	☐
☐	☐
☐	☐
☐	☐
☐	☐
☐	☐
☐	☐
☐	☐
☐	☐
☐	☐
☐	☐
☐	☐
☐	☐
☐	☐
☐	☐

NOTES

March

Year ____________________

SUNDAY	MONDAY	TUESDAY	WEDNESDAY

"We have to do with the past only as we can make it useful to the present and the future."

• Frederick Douglass

THURSDAY

FRIDAY

SATURDAY

NOTES

Week of ___/___/___ to ___/___/___

MONDAY	TUESDAY	WEDNESDAY
☐ ☐ ☐ ☐ ☐ ☐	☐ ☐ ☐ ☐ ☐ ☐	☐ ☐ ☐ ☐ ☐ ☐
☐ ☐ ☐ ☐ ☐ ☐	☐ ☐ ☐ ☐ ☐ ☐	☐ ☐ ☐ ☐ ☐ ☐
☐ ☐ ☐ ☐ ☐ ☐	☐ ☐ ☐ ☐ ☐ ☐	☐ ☐ ☐ ☐ ☐ ☐
☐ ☐ ☐ ☐ ☐ ☐	☐ ☐ ☐ ☐ ☐ ☐	☐ ☐ ☐ ☐ ☐ ☐
☐ ☐ ☐ ☐ ☐ ☐	☐ ☐ ☐ ☐ ☐ ☐	☐ ☐ ☐ ☐ ☐ ☐
☐ ☐ ☐ ☐ ☐ ☐	☐ ☐ ☐ ☐ ☐ ☐	☐ ☐ ☐ ☐ ☐ ☐

THURSDAY

FRIDAY

NOTES

MARCH

Week of ___/___/___ to ___/___/___

MONDAY	TUESDAY	WEDNESDAY
☐ ☐ ☐ ☐ ☐ ☐	☐ ☐ ☐ ☐ ☐ ☐	☐ ☐ ☐ ☐ ☐ ☐
☐ ☐ ☐ ☐ ☐ ☐	☐ ☐ ☐ ☐ ☐ ☐	☐ ☐ ☐ ☐ ☐ ☐
☐ ☐ ☐ ☐ ☐ ☐	☐ ☐ ☐ ☐ ☐ ☐	☐ ☐ ☐ ☐ ☐ ☐
☐ ☐ ☐ ☐ ☐ ☐	☐ ☐ ☐ ☐ ☐ ☐	☐ ☐ ☐ ☐ ☐ ☐
☐ ☐ ☐ ☐ ☐ ☐	☐ ☐ ☐ ☐ ☐ ☐	☐ ☐ ☐ ☐ ☐ ☐
☐ ☐ ☐ ☐ ☐ ☐	☐ ☐ ☐ ☐ ☐ ☐	☐ ☐ ☐ ☐ ☐ ☐

"What is right to be done cannot be done too soon."
• Jane Austen

THURSDAY

FRIDAY

NOTES

MARCH

Week of ___/___/___ to ___/___/___

MONDAY	TUESDAY	WEDNESDAY
☐	☐	☐
☐	☐	☐
☐	☐	☐
☐	☐	☐
☐	☐	☐
☐	☐	☐

THURSDAY

FRIDAY

NOTES

MARCH

Week of ___/___/___ to ___/___/___

MONDAY	TUESDAY	WEDNESDAY
☐	☐	☐
☐	☐	☐
☐	☐	☐
☐	☐	☐
☐	☐	☐
☐	☐	☐
☐	☐	☐
☐	☐	☐
☐	☐	☐
☐	☐	☐
☐	☐	☐
☐	☐	☐
☐	☐	☐
☐	☐	☐
☐	☐	☐
☐	☐	☐
☐	☐	☐
☐	☐	☐
☐	☐	☐
☐	☐	☐
☐	☐	☐
☐	☐	☐
☐	☐	☐
☐	☐	☐
☐	☐	☐
☐	☐	☐
☐	☐	☐
☐	☐	☐
☐	☐	☐
☐	☐	☐
☐	☐	☐
☐	☐	☐
☐	☐	☐
☐	☐	☐
☐	☐	☐
☐	☐	☐

THURSDAY

FRIDAY

NOTES

MARCH

Week of ___/___/___ to ___/___/___

MONDAY	TUESDAY	WEDNESDAY
☐ ☐ ☐ ☐ ☐ ☐	☐ ☐ ☐ ☐ ☐ ☐	☐ ☐ ☐ ☐ ☐ ☐
☐ ☐ ☐ ☐ ☐ ☐	☐ ☐ ☐ ☐ ☐ ☐	☐ ☐ ☐ ☐ ☐ ☐
☐ ☐ ☐ ☐ ☐ ☐	☐ ☐ ☐ ☐ ☐ ☐	☐ ☐ ☐ ☐ ☐ ☐
☐ ☐ ☐ ☐ ☐ ☐	☐ ☐ ☐ ☐ ☐ ☐	☐ ☐ ☐ ☐ ☐ ☐
☐ ☐ ☐ ☐ ☐ ☐	☐ ☐ ☐ ☐ ☐ ☐	☐ ☐ ☐ ☐ ☐ ☐
☐ ☐ ☐ ☐ ☐ ☐	☐ ☐ ☐ ☐ ☐ ☐	☐ ☐ ☐ ☐ ☐ ☐

THURSDAY | FRIDAY | NOTES

MARCH

April

Year

SUNDAY	MONDAY	TUESDAY	WEDNESDAY

APRIL

"For success, attitude is equally as important as ability."
• Harry F. Banks

THURSDAY	FRIDAY	SATURDAY	NOTES

APRIL

Week of ___/___/___ to ___/___/___

MONDAY	TUESDAY	WEDNESDAY

APRIL

SUBJECTS

THURSDAY

FRIDAY

NOTES

APRIL

Week of ___/___/___ to ___/___/___

MONDAY	TUESDAY	WEDNESDAY

APRIL

"Lock up your libraries if you like; but there is no gate, no lock, no bolt that you can set upon the freedom of my mind."

• Virginia Woolf

THURSDAY | FRIDAY | NOTES

APRIL

Week of / / to / /

MONDAY	TUESDAY	WEDNESDAY

APRIL

THURSDAY

FRIDAY

NOTES

APRIL

Week of ___/___/___ to ___/___/___

MONDAY	TUESDAY	WEDNESDAY

APRIL

SUBJECTS

THURSDAY

FRIDAY

NOTES

May

Year

SUNDAY	MONDAY	TUESDAY	WEDNESDAY

MAY

"Whether you succeed or not is irrelevant, there is no such thing. Making your unknown known is the important thing—and keeping the unknown always beyond you."

• Georgia O'Keeffe

THURSDAY	FRIDAY	SATURDAY	NOTES

MAY

Week of ___/___/___ to ___/___/___

MONDAY	TUESDAY	WEDNESDAY

MAY

THURSDAY

FRIDAY

NOTES

MAY

Week of ___ / ___ / ___ to ___ / ___ / ___

MONDAY	TUESDAY	WEDNESDAY

MAY

SUBJECTS

"I avoid looking forward or backward, and try to keep looking upward."

• Charlotte Brontë

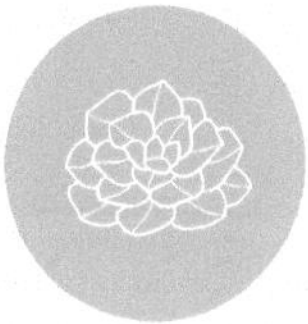

THURSDAY

FRIDAY

NOTES

MAY

Week of __/__/__ to __/__/__

MONDAY	TUESDAY	WEDNESDAY

MAY

SUBJECTS

THURSDAY

FRIDAY

NOTES

MAY

Week of to

MONDAY	TUESDAY	WEDNESDAY

MAY

THURSDAY

FRIDAY

NOTES

MAY

June

Year

SUNDAY	MONDAY	TUESDAY	WEDNESDAY

JUNE

"I never dreamed about success. I worked for it."
• Estée Lauder

THURSDAY	FRIDAY	SATURDAY

NOTES

JUNE

Week of ___ / ___ / ___ to ___ / ___ / ___

MONDAY	TUESDAY	WEDNESDAY

JUNE

THURSDAY

FRIDAY

NOTES

JUNE

Week of ___/___/___ to ___/___/___

MONDAY	TUESDAY	WEDNESDAY

JUNE

SUBJECTS

"The noblest pleasure is the joy of understanding."
• Leonardo da Vinci

THURSDAY

FRIDAY

NOTES

Week of ___ to ___

MONDAY	TUESDAY	WEDNESDAY

THURSDAY

FRIDAY

NOTES

Week of ___/___/___ to ___/___/___

MONDAY	TUESDAY	WEDNESDAY

THURSDAY

FRIDAY

NOTES

JUNE

Week of ___/___/___ to ___/___/___

MONDAY	TUESDAY	WEDNESDAY

THURSDAY

FRIDAY

NOTES

JUNE